WHY SEASONS CHANGE

MARIE ROGERS

PowerKiDS
press™

New York

Published in 2021 by The Rosen Publishing Group, Inc.
29 East 21st Street, New York, NY 10010

First Edition

Editor: Amanda Vink
Book Design: Rachel Rising

Portions of this work were originally authored by Ryan Stark and published as *Why Do Seasons Change?* All new material in this edition authored by Marie Rogers.

Photo Credits: Cover, p. 1 LilKar/Shutterstock.com; pp. 4,6,8,10,12,14,16,18,20,22,23,24 (background) cluckva/Shutterstock.com; p.5 Volodymyr Burdiak/Shutterstock.com; p. 7 janez volmajer/Shutterstock.com; p. 9 Designua/Shutterstock.com; p. 11 zoommachine/Shutterstock.com; p. 13 Andramin/Shutterstock.com; p. 15 Smileus/Shutterstock.com; p. 17 Sergey Novikov/Shutterstock.com; p. 19 Omar Muneer/Shutterstock.com; p. 21 Triff/Shutterstock.com; p. 22 Jenny Sturm/Shutterstock.com.

Library of Congress Cataloging-in-Publication Data

Names: Rogers, Marie, 1990- author.
Title: Why seasons change / Marie Rogers.
Description: New York : PowerKids Press, [2021] | Series: Top-secret nature
  | Includes index. Identifiers: LCCN 2019049449 | ISBN 9781725317611 (paperback) | ISBN
  9781725317635 (library binding) | ISBN 9781725317628 | ISBN
  9781725317642 (ebook)
Subjects: LCSH: Seasons–Juvenile literature.
Classification: LCC QB637.4 .R64 2021 | DDC 508.2–dc23
LC record available at https://lccn.loc.gov/2019049449

Manufactured in the United States of America

Some of the images in this book illustrate individuals who are models. The depictions do not imply actual situations or events.

CPSIA Compliance Information: Batch #CSPK20. For Further Information contact Rosen Publishing, New York, New York at 1-800-237-9932.

CONTENTS

Four Seasons

The four seasons on Earth are spring, summer, fall, and winter. Seasons don't happen the same way in all places around the world. In some parts of the world, **temperatures** change throughout the year. In other parts, they don't.

5

Earth's Movement

Why does Earth have seasons? You may already know Earth orbits, or makes a circle around, the sun. Earth also spins. One full spin is a day. But did you know that Earth isn't **straight** up and down? It's tilted!

Earth's Tilt

Earth's **axis** is tilted, or leaning one way! The tilt makes one part of the Earth point towards the sun, while the other part points away. Earth didn't always tilt. A long time ago, something very big hit the planet and moved it off **balance**.

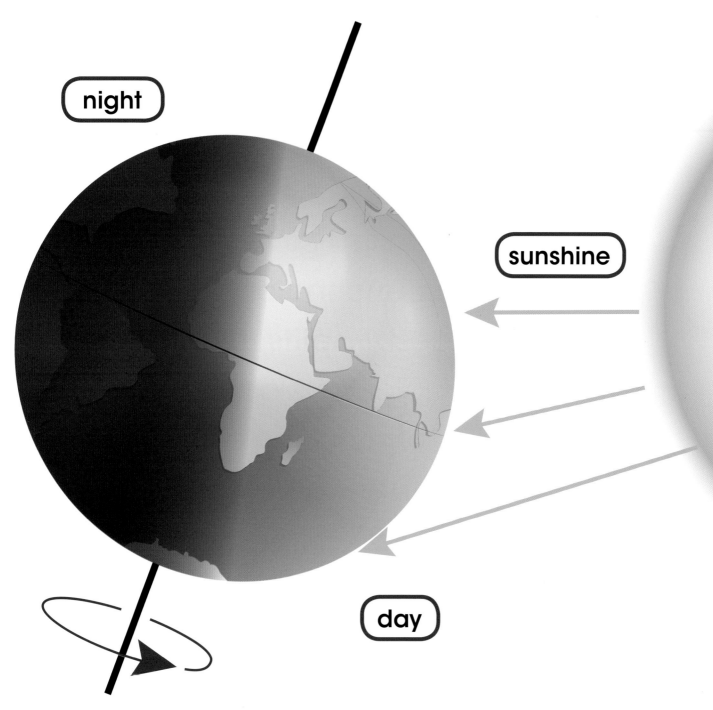

night

sunshine

day

9

The Equator

The equator is an imaginary line that's drawn around the center of Earth at its widest. It **splits** the world in half. The equator gets about the same amount of sunshine every day. Because of that, it's warm there all the time.

equator

Earth's Orbit

It takes one full year for Earth to make an orbit around the sun. During that time, seasons change based on where Earth is located. Each season has things that make it special.

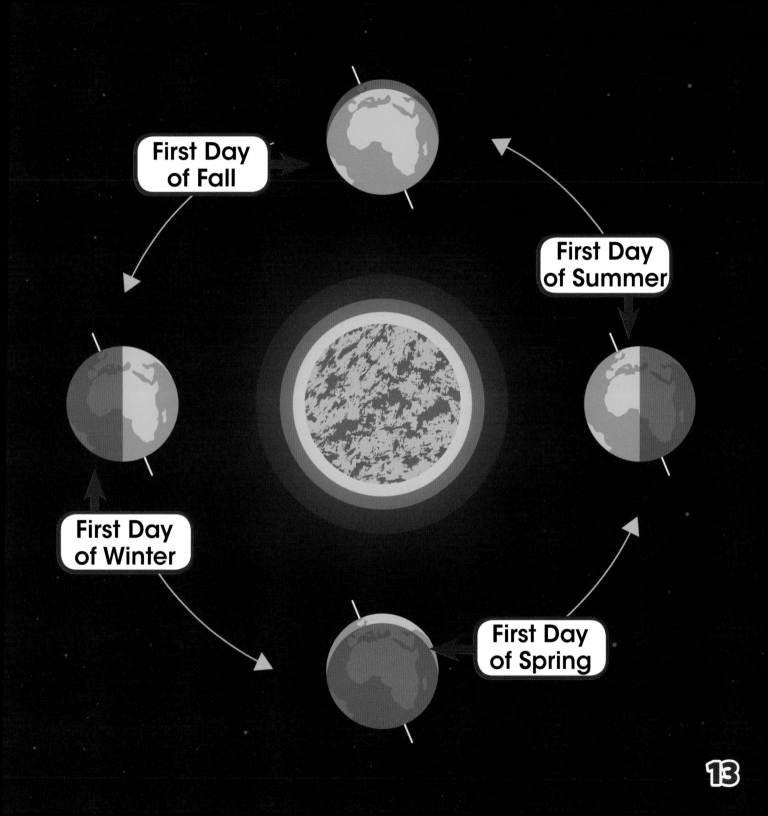

First Day of Fall

First Day of Summer

First Day of Winter

First Day of Spring

13

Spring

As a part of Earth begins to tilt towards the sun, it becomes spring there! Spring is pretty because all the plants start to grow. The area starts to have more daylight every day. The weather also becomes a little warmer every day.

15

Summer

When summer comes, that part of Earth is fully tilted towards the sun. Summer can be hot! The days get longer, and the sun stays out more. Summer is usually a great time to play outside!

Fall

Summer comes to an end when Earth starts to tilt away from the sun. In fall, the days get shorter. It gets cooler. Leaves change colors to red, orange, and yellow. Leaves soon fall from the trees.

Winter

Areas have less sunshine in the winter than in other seasons. That's because that part of Earth is tilted away from the sun. Days are cold and short, and nights are long. Some places get snow, too!

Again!

Once winter is over, spring comes again! The seasons change in order as Earth orbits the sun. Once again there will be spring, summer, fall, and winter. What's your favorite season?

GLOSSARY

axis: The imaginary straight line around which something (such as Earth) turns.

balance: The state in which things occur in equal amounts.

split: To break apart or into pieces.

straight: Not having curves, bends, or angles.

temperature: How hot or cold something is.

INDEX

WEBSITES

Due to the changing nature of Internet links, PowerKids Press has developed an online list of websites related to the subject of this book. This site is updated regularly. Please use this link to access the list: www.powerkidslinks.com/tsn/seasons